W9-ASY-753

THE REVOLUTIONARY WAR

A **TRUE** BOOK

by

Brendan January

Children's Press®
A Division of Grolier Publishing
New York London Hong Kong Sydney
Danbury, Connecticut

American soldiers at Valley Forge

The cover photo shows George Washington crossing the Delaware River with his troops. The title page shows a colonist leaving home to go to war.

Visit Children's Press® on the Internet at:
http://publishing.grolier.com

Library of Congress Cataloging-in-Publication Data

January, Brendan, 1972-
    The Revolutionary War / by Brendan January.
        p. cm – (A true book)
    Includes bibliographical references (p.) and index.
    Summary: Describes the events preceding, during, and following the American Revolution, from the Stamp Act in 1765 to the signing of the treaty in Paris in 1783.
    ISBN 0-516-21630-9 (lib. bdg.)   0-516-27196-2 (pbk.)
    1. United States—History—Revolution, 1775-1783—Juvenile litera-ture. [1. United States—History—Revolution, 1775-1783.] I. Title. II. Series.
E208 .J36 2000
973.3—dc21   99-058707

GROLIER
PUBLISHING

Contents

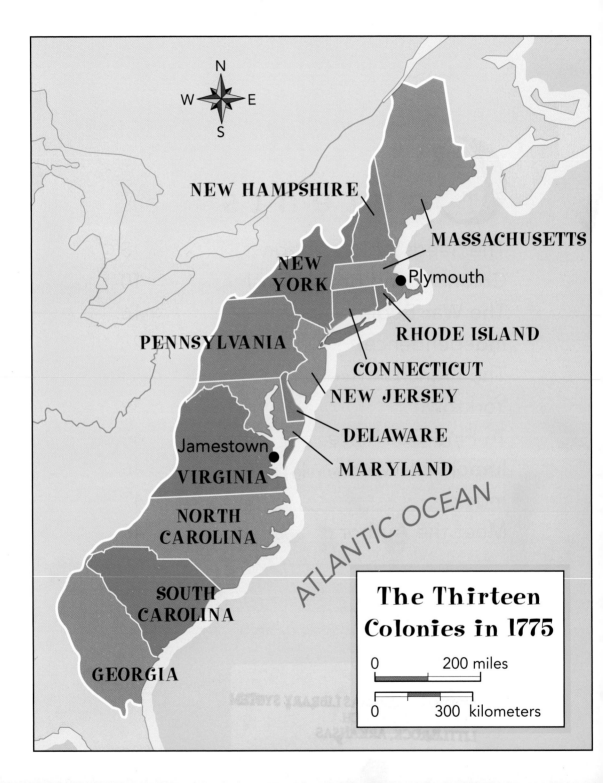

The Thirteen Colonies in 1775

The Seeds of Revolution

In the 1600s and 1700s, thousands of people from Europe came to North America. By 1732, thirteen British colonies stretched along North America's eastern coast. The colonists followed customs and obeyed laws from Europe.

In 1763, the British government needed money to pay its army.

Parliament (a group of leaders that govern England) decided to raise the money by taxing the colonists. In 1765, Parliament passed the Stamp Act. This law said that all printed paper would cost extra money.

The new tax law angered the people in the colonies. The colonists thought it was unfair because they were not allowed to vote on any decisions made by Parliament. The colonists were afraid they might lose their freedom. Colonial leaders sent letters to King George

Colonists burned the tax stamps in the streets of Boston in 1765.

III and Parliament, asking them to remove the hated tax.

Parliament ended the Stamp Act in 1766, and the colonists rejoiced. But in the next year, Parliament passed new taxes on glass, lead, paper, paint, and tea.

A colonist chases away a tax collector.

Again, the colonists protested bitterly. Tax collectors were attacked by angry mobs.

Another popular means of protest was the boycott. In a boycott, people refuse to buy certain goods. In Massachusetts, Samuel Adams led boycotts against British goods.

Samuel Adams urged colonists to stop buying British goods.

The British were shocked. After all, the British had protected the colonies from the hostile French colonists and from the American Indian warriors. The British king and Parliament thought the Americans were acting like ungrateful, spoiled children.

Colonists and British Clash

Boston became the center of the colonial rebellion. In 1768, Parliament sent ships filled with British soldiers to the city. Parliament and King George III thought the army would make the colonists obey their laws.

British troops arrive in Boston to force the colonists to obey British laws.

The army only made things worse. The colonists saw the soldiers as proof that Britain intended to destroy freedom in the American colonies. In the Massachusetts countryside, farmers picked up their muskets and trained themselves to be soldiers. They called themselves "minutemen." If the British army marched, the minutemen

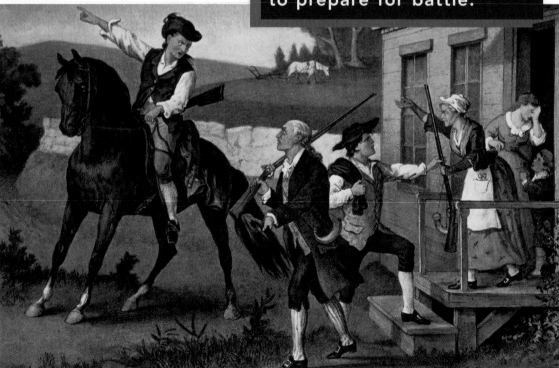

A minuteman gathers other soldiers from their homes to prepare for battle.

could be ready at a minute's notice.

The people of Boston hated having the soldiers in their city. In 1770, an angry mob of colonists threw stones and snowballs at British soldiers. The soldiers panicked and fired into the crowd. Five men were killed, and six were wounded. Colonists called it the Boston Massacre. The British ended the taxes except the one on tea.

Still, the colonists were not happy. On December 16, 1773,

In protest of the tax on tea, a group of colonists dumps tea into Boston Harbor.

a group of colonists dressed themselves to look like American Indians. They rowed out to three British ships in Boston Harbor and dumped all the tea onboard into the water.

14

Parliament and the king were furious when they heard about the so-called Boston Tea Party. They closed Boston Harbor in 1774. Outside Boston, the colonists grew angrier and began collecting guns and gunpowder.

In September 1774, a group of colonial leaders, called the First Continental Congress, met in Philadelphia. They wrote angry letters to the king and Parliament.

The War Begins

General Thomas Gage, the British governor of the Massachusetts Colony, learned that gunpowder was being stored in a town called Concord. On April 18, 1775, he ordered a force of seven hundred men to seize the gunpowder the next day. An

During his ride, Paul Revere rouses colonists from their sleep to warn them of the approaching British troops.

American named Paul Revere heard of the plan. He rode into the night, alerting everyone in the countryside. "The British are coming!" he yelled. Farmers stumbled from their beds and grabbed their muskets.

On Lexington Green, about seventy minutemen waited as the dawn lightened around them. The British would have to pass through Lexington to get to Concord. The American commander, Captain John Parker, warned his men. "Don't fire unless fired upon," he said. "But if they mean to have a war, let it begin here."

A British commander galloped up and angrily ordered the colonists to leave. Behind him, the British soldiers marched into view. Parker realized that he

The battle of Lexington starts with one accidental shot from a musket.

could not defeat such a large force. He ordered his men to scatter. As they obeyed, someone fired his musket. No one knows who fired that first shot. Suddenly, the British guns roared. Eight Americans were killed and ten were wounded.

After being surprised by the minutemen at Concord, the British troops retreat back to Boston.

The British pressed on to Concord. They found few guns and little gunpowder. A colonial force attacked the British soldiers and forced them to retreat. As the British marched back to

Boston, they were fired upon from all sides. Minutemen took aim from behind stone walls and trees. By the time the exhausted British soldiers reached Boston, more than 250 of them had been killed or wounded.

The minutemen followed them. In the hills surrounding Boston, their campfires lit up the night sky. On June 17, British General William Howe ordered more than two thousand men to drive the Americans from

Breed's Hill. On top of the hill, the Americans crouched behind a stone wall and an earthen fort (a fort with walls made of soil) and waited.

The British thought that the untrained Americans would flee. But when the British came near the wall, the Americans fired. At such short range, it was impossible to miss. The British soldiers streamed back down the hill. Soon enough, though, the brave British redcoats formed again and attacked.

Another firestorm of American bullets shattered their lines.

Howe ordered a third attack. As the British approached the earthen fort, only a few shots rang out. The Americans had run out of ammunition. Now the Americans retreated.

The British had taken the hill, but they had also learned that the Americans would fight. More than one thousand British soldiers were killed or injured in that battle.

George Washington became the commander of the American forces in 1775.

The Continental Congress met for a second time in May 1775 to discuss the war. One of the leaders was a man named George Washington. John Adams, a delegate from

Massachusetts, wrote that Washington had a "soldier-like air." The next month, Washington was named commander of the American forces in the Continental Army.

Washington understood the difficulty of winning the war. The powerful British navy ruled the seas. And their army was well equipped and well trained. When Washington took control of the Continental Army, they had few weapons or uniforms.

Independence

In March 1776, the Americans began firing captured British cannons at the British soldiers still in Boston. The British troops boarded their ships and left the city. But Washington remained worried. Where would the British strike next?

In June 1776, a fleet of British ships brought 32,000 soldiers to

General Washington leads the American forces to battle the British and Hessian soldiers.

the outskirts of New York City. Washington rushed his men to meet them. The British and Hessians (German soldiers hired by the British) attacked and drove the Americans out of the city. Defeated, Washington pulled his battered army into New Jersey.

But good news came. On July 4, 1776, the Continental Congress approved a document called the Declaration of Independence. With the words "all men are created equal," the American colonies declared themselves free from Britain.

Still, unless the Americans defeated the British in battle, the declaration was a useless piece of paper. By winter, Washington's men had been defeated on Long Island, New York. They had

The American forces retreat from Long Island, New York, after unsuccessfully fighting British troops.

retreated through New Jersey to Pennsylvania. Snowstorms drenched the frozen and hungry soldiers. Meanwhile, in Trenton, New Jersey, 1,500 Hessian soldiers rested in snug, warm buildings.

In this dark hour, Washington planned his boldest move. After nightfall on Christmas Day, 1776, he loaded his soldiers into boats and crossed the Delaware River. The Continental Army landed in

New Jersey and began marching on Trenton.

In Trenton, the Hessian soldiers were sound asleep when cannon fire shook them from their beds. Out of the morning mist, American soldiers appeared, surprising the unprepared Hessians. Almost one thousand surrendered.

Howe heard of the disaster and rushed British troops to Trenton. But Washington slipped around him and attacked at Princeton. The British retreated again. News spread of the two victories. After a year of defeats, the Americans started to hope.

The French Arrive

The Americans knew that they would need help to defeat the British. They turned to the French, who had fought the British before. American leaders urged them to join the war on their side. But the French needed proof that the Americans could win the war.

In July 1777, British General John Burgoyne led more than 7,700 soldiers into New York from Canada. A second British army would move north from New York City. They planned to meet at Albany. By controlling the Hudson River, the colonies would be cut in half.

The rough wilderness slowed down Burgoyne. No roads existed, and the British soldiers spent days cutting down trees. The army also dragged hundreds of wagons. Burgoyne needed thirty carts to carry his own bags.

Worse, American troops commanded by General Horatio Gates and General Benedict Arnold waited for the British in

Saratoga. Gates ordered seven thousand of his men to dig earthen forts. If the British wanted to continue south, they would have to defeat the Americans first.

Burgoyne ordered his men to attack on September 19 and again on October 7. Both times, the Americans turned them back with heavy losses. On October 17, 1777, Burgoyne surrendered his entire army.

When they heard of this spectacular victory, the French decided

After losing many British soldiers in battle, General Burgoyne surrenders to the American forces.

they could safely support the Americans. They declared war on England on July 10, 1778. Soon, boats filled with supplies and French soldiers were arriv-ing in the colonies.

Valley Forge

The American troops train for battle at Valley Forge.

In September 1777, the British army captured Philadelphia. The Americans retreated and built a winter camp at Valley Forge. For the next six months, the soldiers practiced military exercises in freezing and snowy weather. By spring, the Continental Army was tougher and better trained.

Yorktown

With the French now in the war, the British looked for a new strategy. General Charles Cornwallis decided to strike the southern colonies.

From 1779 to 1780, Cornwallis marched his soldiers through South and North Carolina. He won victories at Savannah and Camden. But the Continental

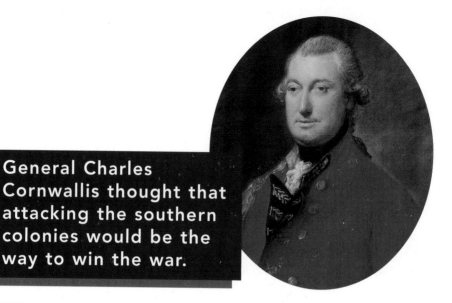

General Charles Cornwallis thought that attacking the southern colonies would be the way to win the war.

Army always challenged his advance. In 1781, he ordered his army north to Virginia. By August, seven thousand British soldiers were camped in the small town of Yorktown, Virginia.

Seeing an opportunity, Washington rushed his army south to Virginia. Suddenly, the British faced an American and

General Washington and French commander Rochambeau observe the British troops from their trenches during the battle at Yorktown.

French army numbering more than sixteen thousand men. Cornwallis, however, did not worry. He thought he could always load his men onto ships and escape. But when French ships arrived and blocked the route, the British were trapped.

For the next two months, the American and French soldiers

General Cornwallis surrenders his army after two months of battling American and French troops.

attacked the British lines. On October 19, 1781, Cornwallis surrendered his entire army. The defeat was a great disaster for the British. When the British soldiers marched out to lay down their guns, a British band played the tune "The World Turned Upside Down." When news of the defeat reached England, a British leader clutched his chest and cried, "Oh God! It is all over!"

Now the British wanted peace. On September 3, 1783, they signed a treaty in Paris. After eight years of bloody war, the colonies were a new nation— The United States of America.

Representatives of the United States and British governments sign the Treaty of Paris, officially ending the Revolutionary War.

To Find Out More

Here are some additional resources to help you learn more about the Revolutionary War:

 **Books**

Davis, Burke. **Black Heroes of the American Revolution.** Harcourt Brace, 1992.

Dolan, Edward. **The American Revolution: How We Fought the War of Independence.** Millbrook Press, 1995.

Grant, Rich. **The American Revolution (Revolution!).** Thomson Learning, 1995.

Kent, Deborah. **The American Revolution: "Give Me Liberty or Give Me Death!".** Enslow Publishers, 1994.

Kent, Deborah. **Lexington and Concord.** Children's Press, 1997.

Lukes, Bonnie. **The American Revolution.** Lucent Books, 1996.

Stein, R. Conrad. **The Boston Tea Party.** Children's Press, 1996.

Stein, R. Conrad. **Valley Forge.** Children's Press, 1994.

Organizations and Online Sites

Colonial Hall: Biographies of America's Founding Fathers
http://www.colonialhall. com/index.asp
This site contains a list and biographies of the men who signed the Declaration of Independence and the Constitution.

The David Library of the American Revolution
P. O. Box 748
1201 River Road
Washington Crossing, PA 18977

Early America
http://earlyamerica.com/ earlyamerica/index.html

Read the Declaration of Independence and other important documents from revolutionary times.

Historic Valley Forge
http://www.ushistory.org/ valleyforge/index.html

This National Historic Site has its own web page filled with information and links.

Liberty! The American Revolution
http://www.pbs.org/ktca/ liberty
This is the companion site to public television's chronicle of the Revolutionary War.

Virtual Marching Tour of the American Revolution
http://www.ushistory.org/ march/index.html

A great site that explores the battles around Philadelphia leading to Washington's retreat to Valley Forge.

Important Words

boycott a type of protest in which people decide not to buy certain goods or products

colony group of people who travel to settle in another land but still obey the laws of their homeland

Hessians soldiers from Germany who were hired to fight the Americans

minutemen colonists who trained to be soldiers and promised to be ready to fight at a moment's notice

musket a heavy shoulder gun with a long barrel

Parliament governing body in England. Leaders are elected or inherit their seat

treaty a document that outlines an agreement worked out between two or more countries or groups

Index

Meet the Author

Brendan January was born and raised in Pleasantville, New York. He attended Haverford College in Pennsylvania, where he earned his B.A. in History and English. He earned his master's degree at Columbia Graduate School of Journalism. An American history enthusiast, he has written several books for Children's Press, including *The Emancipation Proclamation*, *Fort Sumter*, *The Dred Scott Decision*, *The Lincoln-Douglas Debates*, and *The Assassination of Abraham Lincoln*. Mr. January lives in New Jersey and works as a journalist at the *Philadelphia Inquirer*.